Natsuki Hokami

While I was drawing, I remembered something: I really like those jelly drinks that you have to shake. There was a vending machine at the high school I went that sold a mango gelatin in the summer, and I bought a ton of them. I suppose those gelatins are probably gone by now.

Natsuki Hokami's first serialized manga, *Hell Warden Higuma*, was published in *Weekly Shonen Jump* in 2018.

Demon Slayer: Kimetsu Academy

VOLUME 2
SHONEN JUMP EDITION

STORY AND ART BY
NATSUKI HOKAMI

Translation / John Werry
Touch-Up Art & Lettering / E.K. Weaver
Design / Yukiko Whitley
Editor / Andrew Kuhre Bartosh

KIMETSU GAKUEN! © 2021 by Koyoharu Gotouge, Natsuki Hokami
All rights reserved.
First published in Japan in 2021 by SHUEISHA Inc., Tokyo.
English translation rights arranged by SHUEISHA Inc.

The stories, characters, and incidents mentioned in
this publication are entirely fictional.

Printed in the U.S.A.

Published by VIZ Media, LLC
P.O. Box 77010
San Francisco, CA 94107

10 9 8 7 6 5 4 3 2 1
First printing, April 2024

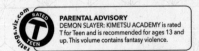

PARENTAL ADVISORY
DEMON SLAYER: KIMETSU ACADEMY is rated
T for Teen and is recommended for ages 13 and
up. This volume contains fantasy violence.

2

The Kimetsu Academy Night Tour

DEMON SLAYER
KIMETSU ACADEMY

Story and Art by
Natsuki Hokami

Based on Koyoharu Gotouge's
Demon Slayer: Kimetsu no Yaiba

KIMETSU ACADEMY

NEZUKO KAMADO

TARO CLASS JUNIOR HIGH, SECOND-YEAR

BAMBOO SHOOT CLASS HIGH SCHOOL, FIRST-YEAR

A serious and polite boy. Wears earrings even though it's against the rules.

TANJIRO KAMADO

Tanjiro's younger sister. Always groggy in the morning.

ZENITSU AGATSUMA

A very moody guy. Part of the disciplinary committee despite Tomioka Sensei's suspicions that his hair is dyed.

BAMBOO SHOOT CLASS HIGH SCHOOL, FIRST-YEAR

A hungry boy who loves tempura. Doesn't bother with books, just his lunch.

INOSUKE HASHIBIRA

BAMBOO SHOOT CLASS HIGH SCHOOL, FIRST-YEAR

HIGH SCHOOL

PEPPER CLASS SECOND-YEAR
MURATA

MUGWORT CLASS THIRD-YEAR
SHINOBU KOCHO

VIOLET CLASS SECOND-YEAR
KANAO TSUYURI

JUNIOR HIGH

TARO CLASS SECOND-YEAR
MAKOMO

TARO CLASS SECOND-YEAR
MUICHIRO TOKITO

TEACHERS

MATH TEACHER
SANEMI SHINAZUGAWA

BAMBOO SHOOT HOMEROOM TEACHER / CIVICS TEACHER
GYOMEI HIMEJIMA

SPARTAN LIFE GUIDANCE / P.E. TEACHER
GIYU TOMIOKA

BIOLOGY TEACHER
KANAE KOCHO

HISTORY TEACHER
KYOJURO RENGOKU

ART TEACHER
TENGEN UZUI

THE STORY SO FAR

Tanjiro and his friends attend Kimetsu Academy, a private elementary, junior high, and high school. The teachers and students are a bunch of weirdos who turn classes into chaos!

GRADUATE / PIZZA DELIVERY GIRL
MITSURI KANROJI

CHEMISTRY TEACHER
OBANAI IGURO

CONTENTS

2 The Kimetsu Academy Night Tour

kimetsu academy!

I LOVE EVERYTHING ABOUT CATS...

...FROM THE WAY THEY LOOK TO HOW THEY BEHAVE.

JUST PETTING ONE IS ENOUGH TO GIVE ME ENERGY BACK.

PURR PURR

...OR FEEDING IT ON SCHOOL GROUNDS, BUT...

SIGH

I KNOW I SHOULDN'T BE CARING FOR IT IN SECRET...

BESIDES, IT'S NOT LIKE ANY STUDENTS WILL FIND ME OUT HERE!

PSS PSS

THIS IS JUST UNTIL YOUR OWNER FINDS YOU!

THEN YOU SHOULD TRY TO FIND ITS OWNER.

WE'LL HELP!

REALLY?

An animal unrelated to your studies? We'll have to blah blah...

...IF TOMIOKA FOUND OUT...

GOOD POINT.

ROCKY

I WAS THINKING OF ROCKY.

TOUGH NAME FOR SUCH A TINY KITTY.

WE CAN COME UP WITH A PLAN AFTER SCHOOL!!

SWISH SWISH

WHAT SHOULD WE NAME IT?

AFTER SCHOOL ...

BAMBOO SHOOT CLASS
FIRST-YEAR

WHOOOA...

I MADE SOME MISSING POSTERS.

FOUNDCAT

DESCRIPTION: CALICO MALE HAS A COLLAR

THIS IS YOUR CAT CALL (XX...

IT'S BORING.

MAYBE A DRAW-ING?

I CAN DO IT!*

HECK NO!

OH, REALLY?

SCOFF SCOFF

YEAH, THIS ISN'T GOING TO WORK.

IT'S ALL WORDS!

IT JUST NEEDS A PICTURE OF ROCKY!

HOW ABOUT THIS PICTURE, THEN?

*CHECK VOLUME 1 TO SEE TANJIRO'S ARTISTIC "SKILLS."

18

THE THREE OF YOU AREN'T SECRETLY KEEPING THIS CAT ON SCHOOL GROUNDS, ARE YOU?

BULLS-EYE

I SAW KAMADO AND HASHI-BIRA...

...PUTTING UP THE SAME NOTICE.

GIYU TOMIOKA
P.E. TEACHER

ZEEEE-NITSUUU!!

I'D NEVER DO SOMETHING LIKE THAT! BUT ONE OF THOSE TWO MIGHT!

W-WHAT? NO! OF COURSE NOT!

...BUT I'M SURE THEY'LL BE FINE.

I TOTALLY SOLD THEM OUT...

PHEW

SKF

THEN I'LL ASK THEM.

OH?

PROB-ABLY.

THANK YOU.

YUSHIRO ?!

TAMAYO SENSEI ... ... AND ...

THEM?

AH!

THE JUNIOR HIGH'S VERY OWN YOKAI...

YEAH, YUSHIRO!!

YOKAI ?!!

...WITH A MONSTER CRUSH ON TAMAYO SENSEI!!

IS THIS CAT YOURS?

WELL, UM...

CHACHA-MARU'S MY CAT.

I SAW YOUR POSTERS.

RUB RUB

...SO HE STARTED COMING EVERY DAY.

...AND HE TOOK A LIKING TO TAMAYO SENSEI...

I BROUGHT HIM TO SCHOOL ONE TIME...

YUSHIRO
GINKGO CLASS
JUNIOR HIGH, SECOND-YEAR

SO HIS NAME ISN'T ROCKY?

HMM...

OH, I SEE.

Sorry for all the trouble.

I CAN'T KEEP HIM IN THE NURSE'S OFFICE, SO I LET HIM OUTSIDE.

33

WELL...

...I'M GLAD WE FOUND YOUR OWNER.

RUB RUB

PURR PURR

THANK YOU FOR MAKING MY DAYS BETTER.

CHACHA-MARU'S A NICE NAME.

POOR SENSEI...

P?!

DON'T BOTHER.

Here.

YOU CAN TAKE HIM HOME NOW.

...

SO WHY WERE YOU CHASING US AROUND?!

REALLY?!

TOMIOKA WAS LENIENT (FOR ONCE).

LOOK THIS WAY, SENSEI!

...THE STUDENTS OFTEN SAW...

AFTER THAT...

...HIMEJIMA PLAYING WITH CHACHAMARU AT SCHOOL.

SNAP

No thanks.

Wanna pet him?

AND THAT'S WHY I KEEP TELLING YOU NOT TO RUN IN THE HALLS!

...COST QUITE A FEW BAGS OF DRIED SARDINES.

THAT SAID, REPLACING THE PHARMACOLOGY CLUB'S SHELVES...

AWESOME ACADEMY

HIMEJIMA SENSEI IS THE BAMBOO SHOOT CLASS'S HOMEROOM TEACHER.

DESPITE THE ACADEMY'S MANY ECCENTRIC STUDENTS...

...HE INSISTS THAT HIS CLASS HAS NO REAL ISSUES.

THAT'S BECAUSE...

EXCUSE ME, SENSEI!

YOU'RE WRITING TOO SMALL! I CAN'T READ IT!

OH, I'M SORRY.

KR

AK

HNGH!

...ANGERING HIM COULD HAVE DISASTROUS RESULTS.

UH, YEAH...

NOW CAN YOU SEE?

But no one has ever seen him angry.

CHAPTER 7: THE SECRET OF HOT SPRING EGGS

OKAY, I'LL TAKE GOOD CARE OF MYSELF.

GOOD LUCK WITH YOUR SUMMER CLASSES.

OH, RIGHT!

DON'T PASS OUT FROM THE HEAT, HISA!

DRINK PLENTY OF WATER!!

CHIR CHIR CHIRR

CHIRR CHIR CHIRR CHIR

I'LL BRING YOU BACK SOME HOT SPRING EGGS.

SEE YOU SOON!

YES, I'LL BRING A LOT.

HOT SPRING EGGS?

So hot!

BETWEEN WORKING OUT AND SUMMER CLASSES...

...THIS ISN'T A BREAK AT ALL!

ZENITSU AGATSUMA
BAMBOO SHOOT CLASS
FIRST-YEAR

UGH...

CHIRR CHIRR CHIRR

WHAT ARE HOT SPRING EGGS?

AND ADDING HOMEWORK IN IS JUST CRUEL!

HM?

WHAT'S UP? WHY'RE YOU SO QUIET?

HEY, MONITSU?

SKREE SKREE CHIR CHIR CHIRR CHIRR CHIR CHIR

CHIRR CHIR CHIR CHIRR

43

TMP TMP TMP

WHY?! CLASS IS ABOUT TO—

FORGET ABOUT CLASS!

NO QUESTIONS!! JUST COME OUT BACK WITH ME!!

WHAT WAS THAT FOR, ZENITSU?!

HE IS?!

INOSUKE'S IN DANGER!!

BUT INOSUKE DIDN'T KNOW WHAT THEY WERE...

...AND SAID SHE'D BRING BACK HOT SPRING EGGS!

TMP TMP TMP TMP TMP TMP TMP

W-WHAT HAP-PENED?!

HISA'S TAKING A TRIP TO A HOT SPRING...

...SO I TOLD HIM!!

"WHAT ARE HOT SPRING EGGS?"

...AND A HOT SPRING GUSHES OUT!!

SPLO DOSH

Here it comes!

HOT SPRING EGG

YOU DIG A HOLE, PLANT ONE...

THEY'RE WHERE HOT SPRINGS COME FROM, DUH.

HOLD ON A SEC!!!

...AND STARTED DIGGING A BIG HOLE!!

THEN HE DECIDED HE WANTED TO PLANT ONE AT SCHOOL...

...

HOT SPRING EGGS! HOT SPRING EGGS!

SHNK SHNK

BY THE TIME HISA GETS BACK...

...I'LL HAVE A GIANT HOT SPRING ALL READY FOR HER!

WHAT DO YOU MEAN?

NOW WHAT, TANJIRO?

DOES HE EVEN HAVE A BRAIN?

I THINK I'M GONNA CRY...

HE'S ACTUALLY DIGGING.

YOU WERE THE ONE WHO LIED TO HIM!!

...BUT I NEED YOU TO BE THE ONE TO TELL HIM THE TRUTH.

Listen... I'LL APOLO-GIZE LATER...

I'LL NEVER ASK ANOTHER FAVOR!

URGH...

NOW YOU GO APOLO-GIZE!

HOP TO IT!

WHAT?! HE'LL KILL ME!

AIN'T THAT GREAT?

DON'T EVEN START WITH ME! I THOUGHT YOU WERE THE HONEST TYPE!!

BESIDES, I REMEMBERED SOMETHING.

WHAT ?!!

I COULDN'T TELL HIM.

BACK WHEN HANAKO WAS LITTLE...

TAKEO SAID A YOKAI INSIDE THE OVEN BAKES THE BREAD.

...TAKEO TOLD HER A BIG FIB.

HANAKO
THE KAMADO FAMILY'S SECOND-OLDEST DAUGHTER

TAKEO
THE KAMADO FAMILY'S SECOND-OLDEST SON

BUT WHEN I TOLD HER THE TRUTH...

Yokai don't actually exist.

SHE WATCHED THE OVEN EVERY DAY, HOPING TO SEE THE YOKAI.

TANJIRO'S FAMILY RUNS A BAKERY.

BA-BMP BA-BMP

...SHE DIDN'T SPEAK TO ME FOR A WHOLE DAY!

PLIP PLIP PLIP

WANNA KNOW SOMETHING NEAT?

I DOUBT THAT!

HUH? NO, UM...

MAYBE WE'LL GET LUCKY AND ACTUALLY FIND ONE!

IT'S ENTIRELY POSSIBLE THERE COULD STILL BE SOME HIDING UNDER-GROUND.

...THIS AREA WAS KNOWN FOR ITS HOT SPRINGS.

BEFORE THEY BUILT THE SCHOOL...

?!

AND VISIT A HOT SPRING AT SCHOOL?!

KIMETSU HOT SPRING?!

WE COULD ACTUALLY SUCCEED?!

THAT MEANS...

WAIT, REALLY?!

YOU'VE NEVER HEARD OF...

...KIMETSU HOT SPRING?

GUYS!

SHINOBU!!

SHINK

GWOOOOO

YES. IT LOOKS LIKE YOU COULD USE A HAND.

YOU'RE ALL HERE TO HELP ME DIG TOO?!

THREE HOURS LATER...

GRRROWL

MAYBE WE NEED MINING GEAR?

NO! WE CAN'T GIVE UP!!

HUFF HUFF

STILL NO HOT SPRING...

NOT EVEN A DROP...

HUH? REALLY?!

HOW ABOUT LUNCH? MY TREAT!

IT'S ALMOST LUNCH TIME.

CLASSES SHOULD BE FINISHING SOON.

GROWL

SO HUNGRY...

THEM

WHAT'S THAT SUP-POSED TO MEAN?!

WHEW! AT LEAST YOU FOUND US...

...AND NOT THEM.

GAH! THERE YOU ARE!!

FORGOT ABOUT THAT.

Oops.

YOU'VE BEEN DITCHING CLASS!!

I'LL GO GET US SOME DRINKS!

CHIRR CHIRR

WELL, IF YOU SAY SO.

Really?

SORRY. I NEEDED THEIR HELP WITH SOMETHING.

I'LL CLEAR IT LATER.

NOW LET'S EAT!!

A HOT SPRING WILL MAKE HER HAPPY TOO!

PSST PSST PSST

I FEEL BAD ABOUT THIS, BUT...

FEEL FREE TO EAT!

OKAY!

PWOK

WE'RE REALLY, REALLY ...

... SORRY !!

INOSUKE ...

COLD

MO TEA

THEY'RE A NATURAL OCCURANCE...

...THAT ONLY APPEAR IN CERTAIN PLACES.

THAT'S WHY THEY'RE SO VALUABLE.

...HOT SPRINGS OCCUR...

...WHEN GEOTHERMAL ACTIVITY HEATS GROUNDWATER.

HOT SPRING

GROUNDWATER

HERE YOU GO!!

MAGMA

67

THEY'RE GOOD FOR BACK PAIN!

REALLY?!

Club prez ↓

BATH SALTS THE PHARMACOLOGY CLUB MADE!

WHAT'S INSIDE?

TAKE THIS AS THANKS!

BUTTERFLY BRAND

SWUP

SHE KNEW WE WERE LYING?!

No way!

HUH?

I'LL BE GOING NOW.

SHE HAD THAT PREPARED.

...

WHAT ABOUT KIMETSU HOT SPRING?

We'll help!

DON'T YOU WANT TO FIND A HOT SPRING?

WHAT'RE YOU TALKING ABOUT?

ARE YOU GOING TO KEEP DIGGING?

NO. I'M LEAVING AFTER I EAT.

WHAT?!

DON'T LEAVE IT TO HER

CHAPTER 8: THE SQUEAL EQUATION

RMBL

KRAKOOM

SANEMI SHINAZUGAWA
MATH TEACHER

GENYA SHINAZUGAWA
CITRUS CLASS
FIRST-YEAR

FREE

RUMBLE

...REDEMPTION VOUCHERS BACK!!

YOU'RE NOT GETTING ...

...YOUR SUMMER FESTIVAL ...

FREE FREE FREE

KRAKOOM

...

YEAH...

FOR FREE GAMES AND STUFF?

VOUCHERS?

Oh!

THAT'S THIS MONTH!

I HEAR YOU!

JUST CALM DOWN AND EAT!

I'VE BEEN COLLECTING THOSE LIKE MAD!!

NO WAY! I REFUSE !!

WHAT WERE YOU PLANNING TO DO WITH 'EM?

WELL, BETTER KISS 'EM GOODBYE.

BUT I DON'T WANNA!!

THE GAME'S OPERATOR WON'T LIKE THAT!

WITHOUT SPENDING ANYTHING?!

MARKS-MANSHIP CLUB ACE →

I WANT TO WIN ALL THE PRIZES AT THE MARKSMANSHIP GAME.

...BUT WHAT WAS YOUR RANK ON FINALS?

I DON'T MIND...

Well...

RIGHT?

ANYWAY, WE'LL HELP YOU.

13/90

THIRTEENTH.

SMARTY-PANTS!

HOW THE HECK ARE WE SUP-POSED TO HELP YOU?!

NO WAY!

ARE YOU FOR REAL?!

GYAH! YOU DON'T UNDER-STAND!

NOM NOM

SALT KOBACHI

SAUCE YAKISOBA

RAMEN

47TH

72ND

28TH

SORRY, AOI!!

ACK!

PIPE DOWN OVER THERE!!

AOI KANZAKI
PERSIMMON CLASS
SECOND-YEAR
(AOZORA DINER
EMPLOYEE)

WELL NOW I'M JUST OFFENDED.

JUST POINT ME AT SOMEONE WHO CAN!

IT WAS MY MATH SCORES THAT WERE THE PROBLEM...

...SO I KNOW YOU CAN'T HELP ME!

NOT HER, IDIOT!!

HEY, AOI!!

LET'S ASK AOI!!

HOW ABOUT AN OLDER STUDENT?

REFILL PLEASE.

YES, INOSUKE?

SO...NOT KANAO OR SHINOBU?

KANAO

SHINOBU

PICK A GUY!

NO GIRLS!

NERVOUS AROUND GIRLS

HMM

HE'S AWAY AT SOCCER CAMP.

SPARKL

6

HOW ABOUT MURATA?

TOKITO

DING DONG

I KNOW!

IT DOESN'T HAVE TO BE AN *OLDER* STUDENT!

HI! I'M HERE TO HANG OUT!!

KO-TETSU?!

HUH?! YOU'RE HERE, TANJIRO?!

KOTETSU
ELEMENTARY SCHOOL, FOURTH-YEAR

SERI-OUSLY?!

I FORGOT WE'D MADE PLANS FOR TODAY.

Thanks.

It's a snack.

MUICHIRO, THIS IS FROM KANAMORI.

CAN WE BORROW THE YOU-KNOW-WHAT?

WE'LL ENLIST HIS HELP AS WELL.

NO.

IF YOU HAVE PLANS, WE CAN—

?

I'D BE DEAD!!!

IT'S GOOD FOR MOTIVATION.

* WATERMELON

...THAT'LL BE YOUR HEAD.

THAT WOULD KILL ME!!

AND WHAT'D YOU DO TO ITS HANDS?!

THAT'S NOT JUST A DOLL, THEN!

YOU PROGRAM IT?!

TAK TAK TAK TAK

I'LL PROGRAM IT TO STOP FOR CORRECT ANSWERS.

HOW IS THAT GONNA MOTIVATE ME?!

I have plenty.

WE'LL JUST HAVE IT SPLIT ANOTHER WATERMELON INSTEAD.

FROM TETSUIDO

OH, OKAY.

TOKITO, I THINK THIS IS A LITTLE TOO DANGEROUS.

...AFTER THE DOLL SPLITS THE WATERMELON...

...I'LL HAVE NO CHOICE BUT TO THROW AWAY THE LEFTOVERS.

OKAY, IN THAT CASE...

CHOMP MUNCH CHOMP

AT THAT POINT YOU'RE JUST WASTING WATERMELON!!

← LOVES WATERMELON

IF THAT'S ALL IT TAKES, WHY'RE WE EVEN USING THAT THING?!

GRAAAAAH

I CAN'T LET THAT HAPPEN!!

THAT'D BE TERRIBLE!!

UM...

SHOULDN'T YOU THREE...

...BE STUDYING TOO?

HUH?

DOESN'T THAT WORRY YOU?

YOUR GRADES ARE WORSE THAN HIS, RIGHT?

YOU GET BAD GRADES WHEN YOU'RE LAZY.

TICK

TICK

TICK

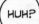
YOU HAVE 20 SECONDS!!

$$y = -3(x-1)^2 + 5$$
$$-3 \leq x \leq -1$$

FIND THE MAXIMUM AND MINIMUM VALUES FOR THIS EQUATION!!

FIRST QUESTION!!

W-WELL, UM...

UM...X=-3 FOR A MINIMUM OF -43 AND X=-1 FOR A MAX OF -7!!!

CORRECT!

...

BESIDES, YORIICHI IS BUSY WITH GENYA.

CHOP

GAH!!

DURING SUMMER BREAK IT IS WISE TO STUDY HARD BUT WHO WOULD BOTHER?

—A SUMMER HAIKU BY THREE NINCOMPOOPS

GENYA'S DEDICATED!

TING
TING

I'M NOT GETTING PUNCHED BY THAT THING!

I DIALED IT DOWN TO GOOSE-EGG MODE.

NO WORRIES! I'VE GOT ANOTHER ONE!!

GAH!

NO WAY!

90

RATL

PIP

TAKING A BREAK, GENYA?

YEAH.

Part-time delivery girl Mitsuru

WE'RE GONNA ORDER PIZZA.

KOTETSU'S RELATIVES RUN A PIZZA JOINT.

SOUNDS GREAT!!

BLEH...

I WAS HOPING I COULD SPEND THE NIGHT TONIGHT...

...SO ABOUT TOMORROW'S BREAD...

REALLY? THANKS, MOM!

I KNOW THAT'S THE RIGHT ATTITUDE, BUT...

Y-YEAH...

LET'S ALL DO OUR BEST!!

DON'T WORRY! YOU'LL GET YOUR VOUCHERS BACK!!

?

HE'S LIKE AN INFORMATION SPONGE.

YOU THINK SO?

...I CAN'T BELIEVE THAT TOKITO...

...ALREADY KNOWS ALL THIS.

IF I WAS GIFTED LIKE TOKITO...

GRRR

You try it!

Come on already!

STAY BACK!

YIIIKES!

Goose-egg mode

CHATTER

C'mon! Just try it!

CHATTER

...THEN MY BROTHER WOULDN'T GET MAD AT ME...

...FOR BEING A LOSER.

HE MUST BE ASHAMED OF ME.

CONTEMPLATIVE

GENYA...

...YOU'RE NOT A LOSER.

HIS FAVORITE?!

YOU'RE HIS FAVORITE!

HE GETS ANGRY BECAUSE HE CARES ABOUT YOU.

...BUT HE'S SUPER HARD ON YOU.

I'VE NEVER SEEN HIM SCOLD ANYONE ELSE FOR THEIR GRADES...

...ISN'T IT?

THAT'S A KIND OF FAVORITISM...

...HAVE A PROBLEM WITH WHAT HE DOES...

BUT IF YOU DO...

IF YOU DO WELL, I BET HE'LL EVEN REWARD YOU!!!

YOU REALLY THINK THAT, HUH?

I'LL BACK YOU UP.

...THEN YOU SHOULD TELL HIM.

AH HA HA HA!

NOT A CHANCE.

STOP GAWKING AT MY TEST!

IT'S NOT JUST A MYTH?!

I DIDN'T KNOW THAT WAS POSSIBLE!

Holy moly!

A HUNDRED POINTS!!

A FEW DAYS LATER...

...OUTSIDE THE SHINAZU-GAWA RESI-DENCE...

SHUT UP!

Move it, Genya!

HURRY!! WE'RE HEADIN' TO THE FESTIVAL!!

URK!

NOW GO INSIDE...

...AND GET YOUR VOUCHERS BACK!

AH!

BOMP BOMP

ARE YOU HERE...?

BIG BRO?

I'M HOME...

WILL HE...

...REALLY GIVE THEM BACK?

CANDIED APPLES!

CHATTER

GENYA! I WANT TAKOYAKI!

CHATTER

GAH! WHAT THE?!

SHAVED ICE!!

YAKI-SOBA!

STOP DROOLING OVER MY VOUCHERS!!

LET'S GO TO THE FESTIVAL!

WHY'RE YOU UP HERE, SANEMI?

SIGH...

AH HA HA HA! AH HA HA! Let's go!

OKAY, OKAY...

THE GUY RUNNING THE MARKSMANSHIP GAME IS THE ONE WHO REALLY WON HERE.

PLAYING AGAIN? THAT'S 300 YEN!

WA HA HA HA

YOU'RE GONNA TAKE ALL THE PRIZES AT THIS RATE!

TOKITOS

CHAPTER 9: THE KIMETSU ACADEMY NIGHT TOUR

IDEAS FOR THE SCHOOL'S SEVEN MYSTERIES?

...PUT OUT A CALL FOR IDEAS!

YEAH! THE SCHOOL PAPER...

Cool!

"ONCE WE HAVE SEVEN, WE'LL ANNOUNCE THE CHOSEN MYSTERIES."

SPOOKY STORIES, HUH?

"...SO WE'RE LOOKING FOR YOUR SPOOKY STORIES."

"LIKE OTHER SCHOOLS, KIMETSU ACADEMY SHOULD HAVE SEVEN MYSTERIOUS HAUNTINGS ..."

IT SAYS, UM...

I BET WE COULD COME UP WITH SOME THINGS!

I'VE NEVER HEARD ANYTHING SPOOKY ABOUT THIS SCHOOL.

THE LEMON-HEADED LUNATIC STALKER!!

HUFF... HUFF... WHERE'S NEZUKO?

SNORT

THE TERRIFYING BOAR-MAN UNDER THE FLOOR!!

THE JUNIOR HIGH'S GOING TO GET IN ON THIS TOO, RIGHT?

I CAN'T WAIT TO SEE WHAT PEOPLE COME UP WITH!

GRAAAH

WHAT'D YOU CALL ME?!

THAT'S WHY WE'LL KEEP IT A SECRET!

WAIT, WE CAN'T! THERE'S NO WAY THE TEACHERS OR OUR PARENTS WOULD LET US!

ADVEN-TURE...

YAY

HMM

TELL YOUR PARENTS YOU'RE SLEEPING OVER AT MY HOUSE!

BRING A FLASHLIGHT AND JUNK FOOD!

...

SABITO
TARO CLASS
JUNIOR HIGH,
SECOND-YEAR

WILL IT BE DANGER-OUS?

COULD BE! THAT'S WHY WE'LL NEED A BODY-GUARD!

YAY! NOW WE'LL BE SAFE!!

WOO WHOO

YAHOO !!

WELL, I GUESS I COULD...

BODY-GUARD

NEZUKO AGREED TO GO.

HM?

...EXCUSE ME?

UM...

YOU CAN INVITE A FRIEND IF YOU WANT!

DON'T BE A SPOIL-SPORT!

BUT ISN'T THIS A BIT KIDDY FOR JUNIOR HIGH?

...AND THIS CLASS WRITTEN ON IT.

I FOUND THIS, AND IT HAD YOUR NAME...

SENJURO RENGOKU
AUTUMN LEAVES CLASS
JUNIOR HIGH, FIRST-YEAR

THE SCHOOL FEELS...

...TOTALLY DIFFERENT AT NIGHT.

IF YOU SEE ONE, MAKE SURE YOU SNAP A PIC!

WELL, THE SCHOOL IS PRETTY OLD!

MAYBE THERE REALLY ARE GHOSTS!

BDMP BDMP

...

AH HA HA HA

WE CAN ASK FOR TWO SELFIES!

SHOULD I ASK PERMISSION FIRST?

OH, RIGHT!

I GUESS EVEN GHOSTS HAVE RIGHTS!

SO WHY'D THEY NEED ME?

THEY AREN'T SCARED AT ALL.

WOO

YAY

I wanna go home...

MAKOMO INVITED HIM.

HUFF HUFF

TRMBL TRMBL

AND WHY'D HE COME?

Yikes! Why're you being so mean?

THEN STOP CLINGING TO ME!

WALK ON YOUR OWN!!

STOP BULLYING HIM, SABITO!

I CAN'T! THIS IS A TEST OF COURAGE FOR ME!

IT'LL HELP ME BE BRAVER!!

IF YOU'RE SCARED, GO HOME.

GWP

SWP

!

SHH!

MAYBE THE SCIENCE ROOM?

SO! WHERE SHOULD WE LOOK?

SWP

SWP

LOOK!

WHAT'S WRONG, SABITO?

SOME-ONE'S IN THE CLASS-ROOM!

WHAT?!

TH-THEN IS THAT...

...A G-G-GHOST?

NO ONE ELSE SHOULD BE HERE THIS LATE!

AH!

WHERE?

YEEEEEEK!

PIPE DOWN.

UM, HE'S...

SO WHO'S THAT KID?

M-MY LEGS GAVE OUT...

ARE YOU ALL RIGHT, SENJURO?

THAT WAS SCARY.

PHEW!

...MY CLASSMATE *RUI AYAKI!*

RUI AYAKI
AUTUMN LEAVES CLASS
JUNIOR HIGH, FIRST-YEAR

WHAT'RE *YOU* DOING HERE?

I JUST DO THIS SOME-TIMES.

WHAT ARE YOU DOING HERE AT NIGHT?

I ENJOY PRACTICING CAT'S CRADLE...

...IN A NICE, QUIET, PEACEFUL ENVIRON-MENT!

BUT UNLIKE YOU, I DON'T MAKE A BUNCH OF NOISE.

DO WHAT?

HANG OUT AT SCHOOL AT NIGHT.

VEEN

SORRY. THEY'RE ALL IDIOTS.

...

CAN YOU MAKE TOKYO TOWER?!

YOU DON'T NEED TO BE SO GRUMPY.

OOH, *ATTITUDE* MUCH?

IF YOU WANT SPOOKS...

...TRY THE HIGH SCHOOL.

NO IDEA.

TMP TMP

CAN YOU S-SENSE SPIRITS?

SERI- OUSLY?

THERE'S A WEIRD FEELING IN THE AIR.

HUH? WHY?

NO.

COME WITH US, RUI!

SHALL WE CHECK IT OUT?

DON'T NEED 'EM.

WE'LL GIVE YOU SNACKS!

AW, C'MON!

THE HIGH SCHOOL

HE'S KIMETSU TOWN'S CAT'S CRADLE CHAMP!

RUI'S KINDA WEIRD, HUH?

...

FUMP

NICE!

WHY ASK ME?

PICKING UP ANY VIBES, SABITO?

HERE WE ARE, BUT...

What should we do?

Hmm...

I NEVER CONSIDERED THAT!

...BUT THE HIGH SCHOOL'S GONNA BE LOCKED UP TIGHT.

I WAS ABLE TO LEAVE ONE OF THE JUNIOR HIGH'S WINDOWS UNLOCKED...

DID SOMEONE JUST OPEN IT?

RATTLE LUCKY US!

HEY! THIS WINDOW'S UNLOCKED!

WHAT'S WRONG, NEZUKO?

HM? WHAT WAS THAT?

OH DEAR...

KYOJURO RENGOKU
HISTORY TEACHER
(SENJURO'S OLDER BROTHER)

YOU'RE HERE TOO, BIG BRO...

IS HE GONNA LECTURE US?!

WHAT ARE YOU DOING HERE AT THIS HOUR?!

...who reaps rice in the home ec room!

The steamy specter..

CAN I TAKE A PIC FOR THE SCHOOL PAPER?

PLEASE DON'T, YOUNG MAN!

YEP!! I'VE GOT THE MUNCHIES!

HERE FOR A LATE-NIGHT SNACK?

BUT WHY SNACK AT SCHOOL?

THOSE GHOSTLY HANDS ARE BECKONING US...

UH-OH...

WHERE'D THE GIRLS GO?

DO YOU DO THIS OFTEN?

"THIS TIME"?

I TRIED COOKING THE INGREDIENTS INTO THE RICE THIS TIME!

THERE! ALL FINISHED!!

WELL, UM...

WHERE DO THE SEALS COME FROM?

SOMEDAY, I WANNA DO AN EXORCISM!

THAT WAS FUN!

YOU DON'T LEARN, DO YOU?

YEAH! A REAL ADVENTURE!

HELP YOURSELF

The night duty room has 'em!!

...I DON'T ACTUALLY KNOW!!

LIKE FREE SNACKS?!

THUS, THANKS TO MAKOMO...

Wow!

THEY MUST BE FROM A FAMOUS SHRINE!

STAFF

THEY KEPT THE NIGHT GUARD SECRET, THOUGH.

SEVEN SCHOOL

KIMETSU ACADEMY

..."THE CREEPY OLD BABY GUY" AND "THE GUY IN A POT"...

...WERE ENSHRINED AS TWO OF THE SCHOOL'S SEVEN MYSTERIES.

KOCHO SENSEI!

ARE YOU USING THE COPY MACHINE?

YES?

YES, I AM.

KANAE KOCHO
BIOLOGY TEACHER

...

NO, BUT...

DO YOU NEED TO USE IT?

Right?

IT BEATS WRITING THEM BY HAND!

TEE HEE!

??

THE SOURCE OF THE SEALS WAS CLOSE AT HAND.

GWOOOO

...WHAT ARE YOU COPYING?

OH, THAT?

LIFE IN TARO CLASS

CHAPTER 10: LOVE AND SNAKES

NO FREAKING WAY...

IT'S FOR...

CHEMISTRY

WAG WAG

Oh, you forgot your homework?

NOT A CHANCE!

WELL, I GUESS HE'S POPULAR!

HE'S A GLOOMY AND ANNOYING SNAKE!!

Then why even bother coming?!

ROMANCE ISN'T A COMPETITION! BE STRONG, ZENITSU!

HE BEAT ME!!

I CAN'T BELIEVE IT!!

FINE, WHATEVER. BUT...

...OBANAI IGURO?! OUR CHEMISTRY TEACHER?!

OBANAI IGURO
CHEMISTRY TEACHER

HELP ME FIND A PRESENT FOR KANROJI.

I'M TALKING TO YOU TWO.

OKAY, BUT...

...WHY ARE YOU ASKING US?

I WANT TO GIVE HER A GIFT, BUT I DON'T KNOW WHAT.

KANROJI AND I ARE PLANNING TO HAVE DINNER TOGETHER.

LISTEN TO US!

WE FORGOT ALL ABOUT THAT!!

HUH?! ARE YOU SERIOUS RIGHT NOW?!

EEK!

KANROJI WENT TO SCHOOL HERE, RIGHT?

EVERYONE WHO KNOWS HER RECOMMENDED FOOD.

WHY NOT ASK THE OTHER TEACHERS?

*IGURO DIDN'T START WORKING HERE UNTIL AFTER SHE GRADUATED.

I WOULD RATHER NOT INVOLVE STUDENTS BUT...

...YOU'RE THE ONLY ONES I CAN TRUST WHO KNOW ABOUT THIS.

WE ALWAYS GO OUT TO EAT, SO I NEED SOMETHING BESIDES FOOD!

WHAT'S WITH THE LOOK?

DOES HE...NOT HAVE ANY NON-WORK FRIENDS HE COULD ASK?

SURE! I'D BE HAPPY TO!!

WHAT?!

WHY SHOULD I CARE...

...ABOUT SOME OTHER GUY'S DATE GOING WELL?

WHAT'S THE PAY LIKE?

I WILL...?

YEAH! ZENITSU WILL HELP TOO!!

REALLY?

I *SHOULD* REPAY YOU SOMEHOW...

HOW ABOUT I BUY YOU LUNCH?

But keep it secret.

THEN WHY SHOULD I— UGH!

HMM...

HE DOESN'T HAVE TO PAY US!!

FREE LUNCH? I'M IN!!

NO!!!

I'LL TREAT YOU TO WHATEVER YOU WANT.

INOSUKE HASHIBIRA
BAMBOO SHOOT CLASS
FIRST-YEAR

KYAH!!

...BUYING A PRESENT FOR ME?!!

SHE FIGURED IT OUT INSTANTLY!

OH!

AN ACCESSORY SHOP?

Care SHOP

COULD HE BE...

T FOR YOU

US ON 2F →

IN THE SHOP...

I'M SUPER EMBARRASSED TOO!

TMP

NO WONDER HE'S SO NERVOUS!

UH, Y-YEAH...

WILL YOU BE ALL RIGHT, SENSEI?

THERE'RE SO MANY GIRLS!

GUH!

WE'RE HERE BECAUSE OF YOU!!

P'BOOM

YOU'RE PRETENDING WE'RE STRANGERS?!!

HOWEVER...

THAT SETTLES IT! NOW—

HOW ABOUT A HAIR ORNAMENT, SENSEI?

HMM...

I BET THIS ONE'D LOOK GOOD ON KANROJI.

SHE'LL BE WEARING IT AROUND OTHER PEOPLE, SO IT'S MORE IMPORTANT...

...WHETHER IT'S TO HER TASTE.

I WOULDN'T WANT HER TO FEEL OBLIGATED TO WEAR SOMETHING SHE DIDN'T LIKE.

YES, IT WOULD...

GWOOOOOOO

THE ROAD AHEAD LOOKED LONG.

...

STMP

I'LL THINK ABOUT IT.

ON TO ANOTHER SHOP.

IT'S PAST NOON.

Nope...

No...

Not this one...

Not this one either...

IF HE ASKED FOR OUR HELP...

...HE MUST BE SERIOUS ABOUT THIS.

IS SHOPPING FOR GIRLS REALLY THAT HARD?

What a pain!

WE HAVEN'T MADE ANY PROGRESS ALL MORNING!

ARE YOU EVEN TRYING?!

SHALL WE BREAK FOR LUNCH?

I'LL DECIDE THIS AFTERNOON.

FAMILY RESTAURANT

FAMILY RESTAURANT

Welcome!

HONESTLY, I PREFER FINER DINING...

DOES THIS PLACE WORK FOR YOU?

YEAH! THE MENU'S GOT VARIETY!

WHOA

LET'S DIG IN!!

MNCH NOM MNCH

HERE YOU GO!

HAMBURGER STEAK, GRILLED EEL, AND FRIED CHICKEN!

....!!

NO WAY! IT'S HIDEOUS!

GUY'S GOT NO FASHION SENSE! WA HA HA!

YEAH!! MY BOO BOUGHT THIS BAG FOR ME!!

REALLY, HEBIKO?!

DON'T WORRY.

UM, IGURO SENSEI?

HM?

I'M FINE.

KANROJI ISN'T LIKE THAT.

DO THEY HAVE TO BE...

...SO LOUD?

HE EVEN SAID HE SPENT ALL DAY PICKING IT OUT!!

EW! CREEPY!!

TITTER TITTER GIGGLE GIGGLE GUFFAW

...

Thanks for coming in!

FAMILY RESTAURANT

WELL, IF YOU'RE SURE...

NO, NOT AT ALL!!!

HM...

BUT... AM I CREEPY TOO?

...some eats!

I love me...

WHAT KANROJI LIKES IS OBVIOUS...

...SO I SHOULD GET HER SOMETHING SWEET.

YOU'RE DOING FINE!!

NO...

...I'M OVER-THINKING THINGS.

GLASSES

OFF-SEASON, LIMITED-QUANTITY, *HYPER SAKURA MOCHI!!*

THIS PLACE IS ADVERTISING A GORGEOUS JAPANESE CONFECTION!!

AHA!

A TREAT, HUH?

CHATTER CHATTER CHATTER

LET'S GO STRAIGHT THERE!!

KANROJI DOES LIKE SAKURA MOCHI.

DADOOM ...!!

BDMP

BOMP

...!!

SENSEI! CAN YOU DO IT?!

THE LINE IS NUTS!

AND THEY'RE ALL GIRLS!

WE'LL GET IN LINE FOR YOU, SENSEI!!

DASH

THEY'RE GONNA RUN OUT!

SHF SHF

OH NO!

THE LINE'S GETTING EVEN LONGER!

WE'RE ALMOST THERE!

ONLY 20 MORE PEOPLE!

HUFF HUFF

YOU CAN DO IT, TEACH!

CLMP

NO...

...I HAVE TO DO THIS MYSELF!!

FIVE!

JUST TEN MORE!

WE'RE NEXT!!

SWP

SO

I'M COMPLETELY FINE AROUND HER.

YES. ISN'T THAT ODD?

YOU'RE UNCOMFORTABLE AROUND GIRLS...

...BUT YOU'RE OKAY AROUND KANROJI?

Oh my!

Sorry!

I GET ALL ANXIOUS AROUND OTHER GIRLS AND MAKE THEM UNCOMFORTABLE.

I'M AWARE OF HOW PATHETIC IT IS.

YEAH?

Nezukooo!

...I FORGET ALL THAT AND JUST ENJOY MYSELF.

BUT WHEN I'M WITH KANROJI...

I COULD BARELY LINE UP TO BUY MOCHI.

...SO I WANTED TO DO THE SAME FOR HER.

SHE GIVES ME SO MUCH...

SNAKE SCARF

SHE GAVE ME A BIRTHDAY PRESENT THE OTHER DAY.

SORRY FOR BOTHERING YOU TWO WITH THIS.

HUH ?!

SWIP

OH WELL. LET'S GO HOME.

IT WAS JUST SOMETHING I WANTED TO DO.

BUT WHAT ABOUT A PRESENT ?!

"THANKS SO MUCH, ZENITSU!"

"IT WAS TASTY!"

THIS ISN'T A SPECIAL OCCASION.

I'LL GET HER SOMETHING SOME OTHER TIME.

MOPING DOESN'T SOLVE ANYTHING!

YOU'VE GOTTA SHOW YOUR FEELINGS!!

Z-ZEN-ITSU?

YOU HAVE TO GIVE HER A PRESENT!!!

BECAUSE PRESENTS...

...ARE GOOD FOR BOTH THE GIVER AND THE RECEIVER!!

EVEN IF IT'S JUST FOR YOU, YOU'VE GOT TO GIVE HER A PRESENT!!

YEAH! LET'S KEEP LOOKING!

AGA-TSUMA...

HUFF HUFF

BY THE WAY...

...I BROUGHT SOMETHING FOR YOU.

RUSTL

OH?

I LOVE HAVING DINNER WITH YOU!!

OPEN IT UP.

I HAD NO IDEA!

A PRESENT?! WHAT A SURPRISE!!

OOH! WHAT CUTE SOCKS!

I HAD TO GO TO WORK ...

...SO I HAVE NO IDEA WHAT IT IS!

TEE HEE HEE!

B DMP B DMP

AND THEY'VE GOT—!

BIG HAND CAT IS AN ORIGINAL CHARACTER...

...THAT KANROJI DESIGNED AS AN ART STUDENT.

Lookie, Iguro!

I SEARCHED ONLINE FOR A SHOP...

...THAT WOULD EMBROIDER THEM BASED ON YOUR ILLUSTRATION.

SHF

I ALSO HAD THEM EMBROIDER...

...SOMETHING FOR ME.

I WANTED TO DO IT MYSELF, BUT IT WAS TOO DIFFICULT.

This place'll do it!!

Here, Sensei!!

...

...TO MATCH YOUR SOCKS.

FWIP

A HANDKER-CHIEF...

?!

PLIP

... BUT ...

IT'S STRANGE.

I WANT MY ART TO MAKE THE WORLD HAPPY...

IGURO... I, UM...

K...

KAN-ROJI?

...RIGHT NOW...

...IT'S MAKING ME THE HAPPIEST OF ALL!

OH...

THAT'S GOOD.

IGURO...

...WOULD GO ON TO BE MUCH KINDER TO TANJIRO AND ZENITSU.

I'M GLAD.

...A CROW CARRYING A LOVE LETTER...

BUT NOW WHEN THEY SEE...

...THEY CAN'T HELP BUT SMILE.

JUST KIDDING!

NO NAP-PING IN CLASS!

CHAPTER 10 DELETED SCENES
USELESS TEACHERS

Kanroji in high school

Q. **WHAT WOULD MAKE A GOOD PRESENT FOR KANROJI?**

I NEED HELP

HIMEJIMA SENSEI SUGGESTED THE OBVIOUS.

...SO MAYBE FOOD?

SHE ONCE BROUGHT A WHOLE STACK OF BOX LUNCHES...

FOR KANROJI?

That made an impression!

SHINAZUGAWA SENSEI GAVE IT MINIMAL THOUGHT.

MAYBE JUST ONE BIG BOX LUNCH INSTEAD?

KOCHO SENSEI'S IDEA WAS ROMANTIC (BUT UNREALISTIC.)

YOU COULD GROW FLOWERS THERE! HOW ROMANTIC!

BUY HER A FRUIT FIELD! SHE'D LOVE THAT!

UZUI WENT FOR STEREOTYPES.

SO TREAT HER TO A FINE MEAL!!

COLLEGE KIDS ARE POOR!!

HAGANEZUKA SENSEI RECOMMENDED THINGS HE WANTS.

A GRINDSTONE.

GOTO PLAYED IT CASUAL.

SHE'LL LIKE ANYTHING YOU GET HER.

KYOGAI SENSEI WAS THOUGHTFUL.

...SO STUFF HER WITH FOOD.

SHE CAN'T BUY FROM THE SCHOOL KIOSK ANYMORE...

DESPITE BEING HER FORMER TEACHER, RENGOKU WAS STILL RENGOKU.

HOW ABOUT A BAG OF RICE?!

HE DIDN'T BOTHER ASKING TOMIOKA SENSEI.

THAT EXPLAINS IT.

...

WHICH ONLY LEFT...

VOLUME 2 (END)

くもとり
KUMOTORI

TANJIRO ALWAYS CATCHES HIM MIS-BEHAVING ON THE TRAIN.*

HE'S A TRAIN GEEK WITH A CRIMINAL HABIT.

*SEE VOL. 1, CHAPTER 1.

THIS IS TAMIO ENMU.

*EYES: LOWER ONE

BONUS CHAPTER: KUMOTORI STATION, 7:30 A.M.

...

TMP
TMP
TMP

くもとり
KUMOTORI

175

I'M TAMIO ENMU. NICE TO MEET YOU.

THE NAME'S TANJIRO KAMADO!

UM, EARRING BOY...

WHY CAN'T I DISROBE ON THE TRAIN?

BAM

BECAUSE OF BOX LUNCHES!!

HMM... I NEVER CONSIDERED THAT.

AND THAT'S A PROBLEM!

NOW YOU KNOW!

...THEY'LL FORGET ABOUT THEIR LUNCHES WHEN THEY RUN!

IF YOU SCARE THE PASSENGERS...

WHAT?

Eek! A butt!

AFTERWORD

Welcome to volume 2! Thanks for reading! Just like with volume 1, this was only possible through the efforts of a lot of people, so thank you all very much. I'll be counting on you in the future too.

This volume goes on sale in July, and the story takes place from early summer to autumn, so I'm thrilled to see how the seasons have synced up. What a happy coincidence!

The serialized releases never match the actual season, so I drew the preceding two-page spread to match with the real world. Without any connection to the story, the sakura trees are in full bloom! I have to say, I like that illustration, but I was never satisfied with the color illustration of Makomo and the others for chapter 9, so I put them on the back cover of this volume.

I suspect volume 3 will take place from autumn to winter. Nothing is slated yet, though, so here's hoping it gets the green light!

STAFF

REGULARS
Nagashima
Kantaro Kumano
Keisuke Futta

HELPERS
Kojiro
Tachi Biwa

SPECIAL THANKS
Saikyo Jump editor: Toide-san
The *Demon Slayer: Kimetsu no Yaiba* original manga team
Graphic novel editor: Abe-san
Designers: Deguchi-san, Abe-san
Original creator: Koyoharu Gotouge
All the readers!

Natsuki Hokami

帆上夏希.

Good work! This is Gotouge! Volume 2 of *Kimetsu Academy* is on sale! Here's a big thanks to Hokami Sensei, the editors, assistants, and readers! The number of characters playing a role is ramping up, making these pages more boisterous than ever!

As the fun continues to take off, I hope you'll come along for the ride!!

FIRST-YEAR TEXTBOOK DESIGNS
FOR KIMETSU ACADEMY HIGH SCHOOL

For a while, I only had a rough idea for these,
but I asked my staff and they came up with proper designs.
The other grades basically look the same.

You're reading the wrong way!

In keeping with the original Japanese comic format, *Demon Slayer: Kimetsu Academy* reads from right to left, meaning that action, sound effects, and word-balloon order are completely reversed from English order.

Check out the diagram shown here to get the hang of things, and then turn to the other side of the book to get started!